Cultural Women

A Coloring Book of 23 Women in Their Traditional Dress From Around the World

----

I dedicate this book to Leia, Suzanne, Jill and Kate.

ಐ*ಞ

Created By: Kristen Carlson

9/30/2015

Made in United States
North Haven, CT
22 September 2021